NINE SERI

All About Our

Vasiliki Albedo
Mary Mulholland
Simon Maddrell

Published by Nine Pens
2022
www.ninepens.co.uk

All rights reserved: no part of this book may be reproduced without the publisher's permission.

The right of the author(s) to be identified as the author(s) of this work has been asserted by them in accordance with the Copyright, Designs and Patents Act 1988

ISBN: 978-1-7398274-0-3

NS 001

Vasiliki Albedo
- 7 Pine Summit
- 8 I watch a bear eat her sick cub
- 10 Hard-boiled
- 12 I tell my mother I'd rather stand outside all night than go to sleep and she lets me
- 13 Butterfly mother
- 14 Therapy Cat
- 15 Mother in fur
- 17 Last Day
- 18 Encore

Mary Mulholland
- 23 Things Our Mothers Couldn't Teach Us
- 24 Behind the Glass
- 25 Fault-lines
- 26 Mother's Child
- 28 Comb
- 30 The art of daydreaming
- 32 The sea is sleeping
- 33 Daisy ring
- 34 The Canal du Midi where I find my mother

Simon Maddrell
- 39 There was a hole
- 40 Only a Mother can look with
- 41 Alright really
- 42 She never came unannounced
- 44 Rabbit-shocked
- 46 Penny
- 47 Kipper
- 48 Elegy
- 49 The church's oak creaks into silence

Vasiliki Albedo

Vasiliki Albedo's poems have appeared in *Anthropocene, AMBIT, Beloit Poetry Journal, Lighthouse Literary Journal, Magma, The Rialto, The Morning Star, Poetry Salzburg Review, Mslexia, Poetry Wales* and elsewhere. In 2017, she came second in the Oxford Brookes International Poetry Competition (EAL) and joint-third in the Brian Dempsey Memorial Prize. Nominated for Pushcart Prizes, Vasiliki was joint-winner in the Guernsey International 'Poems on Buses' in 2021, commended in the National Poetry Competition 2018 and the Hippocrates Prize 2021. *Fire in the Oubliette* was joint-winner of the Live Canon Pamphlet Competition 2020. She is a member of The Crocodile Collective.

Pine Summit

In this picture I'm propped on her
shoulders and she's shooting
my one-year-old arms
to a needled sky
as if to sign *Victory*.
My fists are out of sight
inside her fingers,
her bronze jersey's tarnished
with mud from my booties
as I crown her head.
Our outstretched arms
form a U and a Y
into my father's unfocused
camera as I look into the distance
and my mother beams face-on,
her hair shades darker
than my own flyaway
curls, not yet the violent
red of my jacket, but a pale
orange flame, taking hold.

I watch a bear eat her sick cub

At home water is forbidden.
Mother says I must only have milk.
She believes it's a panacea
for failing, sulky girls.

But secretly I drink the faucets dry.
Mother suckles her cherub,
my little brother, gives me cartons
of curdy, Dutch milk.

She offers her green, gigantic breast,
asks me if I'm jealous.
Her milk is pink with blood and pus.
Nights, I bite holes

into the dress she makes me wear.
When she tugs the neckline shrieking
I whisper that my brother did it.
Drink the milk, she says

it'll make you taller,
and I raise another fever.
Once, I too suckled,
felt the syrup sour on my tongue.

Now I sweeten at a distance.
She bolts me in my room.
The cold season snaps
heads off statues in the park

where she walks with my brother
in her arms. I make it rain as I stare
at them through the window.
My heart ripens like a nightshade.

Hard-boiled

I want it as it is, not fried.
Fine, she replied, smashing it

against the rim. Was I a bad egg?
Blended, broken yolk and see-through slime,

she put the raw mess down,
not the boiled version I'd had in mind.

So I'd been wrong. Under her stare
was forced to eat it all, no matter

if I pleaded, if I retched. Even then
I knew what she meant to teach me,

but that egg was my first taste
of something else. Now when I binge

on Criminal Confessions I still believe
they are all innocent:

the good-natured lawyer who cinched
a belt around his girlfriend's neck,

dragged her behind his car,
pummeled her to death

with a pump. The pious family
man who swore he knew nothing

about his ex-wife's end,
but had in fact spent a month

buying supplies: the bat, the axe,
the acid. The smart, talented

boy who strangled his friend
in the backseat of his car

for thirteen minutes
(he was looking at the watch). He said,

he got what he'd asked for.

I tell my mother I'd rather stand outside all night than go
to sleep and she lets me

The tiles were hot all through the night.
I stood, locked out, back up against
the poxy, clapboard bungalow,
counting hours, counting stars.
First light she came for me,
dragged me to her fuggy, violet room,
slapped then said she would not slap me
anymore, now I was eight, she could
end up in jail, and barked
you look me in the eye.
I drew my gaze from her forehead
down to her deep mahogany stare
and the crystal angels on her dresser
spun, as my palm rose
to smart her cheek, just once.

Butterfly mother

In her mirror the night was a cocoon
winging my eyes, defining. Her foundation
slipped on my skin, making me golden.
It was a trap. Caterpillar brows plucked,
my invisible veins ruptured for her
tender cottonwool dab.

She shaded the tip of my nose,
joked, feathered the rouge
till my temples incarnadined.
The painted pattern filmed
over the house she and I lived
with her cupboards of creams,
her lipsticked smile, and chrysalis eye.

Later it bittered when I wore glasses
she said didn't flatter, and my spiteful
haircut pierced her fingertips.
My colours churned in her then mottled.
My pouch-like clothes flopped
against her iridescent dresses.

She put my portrait in the shed.
I looked sad, she said. She left
only one image in her locket:
my raw, newborn face.

Therapy Cat

The lame cub a lioness left to the eagles took me
back to my eighth birthday and the analyst's gift
of a piebald kitten. She called it *a therapy cat* but
my mum confined it to the second-floor balcony:
IT'LL RUIN THE HOUSE, IT'LL RUIN THE HOUSE.
Each night when I slept she'd toss it out, and each morning
I'd pick it out of a pot in the garden, limping and frightened:
LET IT GO, IT WANTS TO GO BACK TO ITS MOTHER.

At thirteen I came home from school to find
my room arranged into my brother's:
I THREW OUT YOUR THINGS, STAY AT YOUR FATHER'S.
For years I dreamed therapy cat had morphed
into a winged lioness, her limbs whole and inviolate.
We'd meet in my room and ride into a fictive sunburst.
And in that light, there was nowhere that wasn't home.

Mother in fur

On the news, the open-faced
close up zooms me back

to my childhood. The anchor
is speaking but it's my mother

she is reciting as she reports on the war
and someone mauled at the zoo.

She blinks, and her eyes are an event
horizon from which my mother backflips.

She appears in my bedroom, fully
made up, in her freshly-skinned coat

and Marilyn-Monroe mole.
She sways past me,

into a flamboyant skyline
where her cigarette lights clouds on fire.

After commercials, she's back
in the anchor's fresh lipstick coat.

When she enters the room it feels
as if there's just been a murder

for which no one will ever be charged.
The anchor wishes us a good evening

and presents the aftermath
of the latest bomb strike.

Years ago, I was at school
when mother paid me a visit,

saying she'd missed me,
stamped a kiss on my lips,

caressing my cheek with her diamond
when she was wearing nothing

under her fur and only came
to meet the headmaster I had a crush on.

In other news, a hurricane
is heading our way.

The anchor advises: seal
all windows, and shelter.

Last day

The morphine-drip tides you quiet and I sit on the hospital steps.
Seven years of cancer and still we haven't reconciled.

How many times I've sat on the granite blocks outside
our complex, locked out, not knowing where you are or if

you're coming back. And when you did, slurring apologies,
I'd wipe your salting makeup, cook you breakfast.

Remember that Christmas when you gave me a shawl for the cold
and a letter from Santa that listed the ways I had upset you?

For days you have been talking to your dead mother.
I overheard your conversations, how you said

you don't want to leave me, said you can't forgive me.
I never told you about the neighbour who took me in

when it was raining, made me eggs and gave me keys
to her apartment. How I grew there.

Soon, I will come into the ward, cup your hand,
take the oxygen mask away to let you kiss me.

I love you, I'm sorry echoing between us.

Encore

But now you're gone,
birds clap the sky for an encore,

mother, and look what you've done
to the sea.

Fish worry her surface
and never again will sleep.

In my window
the sun is a blind

rising and falling,
trapped in-between.

Mary Mulholland

Mary Mulholland's poems have been widely published in magazines such as *AMBIT, Arc, Fenland Poetry Journal, Finished Creatures, High Window, London Grip, Perverse, Snakeskin, Under the Radar,* and in several anthologies. Twice-winner in Poetry Society Members' competitions, she also won the Momaya Poetry Prize, and been commended or shortlisted in competitions including AMBIT, Aesthetica, Artlyst, Aryamurti, Bridport, Trim, Wasafiri, Winchester and Live Canon Pamphlet Prize. Mary holds a Newcastle/Poetry School MA in Writing Poetry, co-edits *The Alchemy Spoon,* runs Red Door Poets and is a founding member of The Crocodile Collective.

Things Our Mothers Couldn't Teach Us

One last bend of the five-hour drive
in a November storm. My headlights flash
on a quivering scrap, mossy grey-brown,
the wrong shape for a rat. I step into rain,
the voice in my head says, find a stone.
I raise my arm to its near-lifeless form.
It blinks. I crouch down, lift it, the size
of a hand and half of that is ear.
Ludicrous ears. Sodden fur.
I stroke it: a tremor, a mothwing
heart in a still pool. I was told
the cry of a dying hare echoes our soul.
How does anyone tune into their leaden?
Hares are self-sufficient from birth,
but must learn self-defence, to box
and run zigzag. Their mothers can't help:
jills are busy with their moon-living
pounding a mixture for immortality.

So many cars speed by, but I stay
until the rain stops. I'm wet through.
The leveret is warmer, it's moving.
I lay it on the verge below the hedgerow,
return in the morning. No sign it was there.

Behind the Glass

Ours was not a vain house. Mirrors reserved
for the bathroom. Except one my mother had,
hand-held silver-framed. I can see her lost
in gazing at it, would try to squeeze in, share
her reflection: with her pale skin & night-
black hair, she was a young Elizabeth Taylor.
Big baby, she'd say & put away her mirror
face, looking at me in a less beautiful way.

No polishing could control the ageing, but
after she died I held her silver mirror to see
what had so captivated her, stared closer &
closer until my hazel eyes turned her dark,
saw a stranger, unsure which side was me.

Fault-lines

Everywhere I hear it in the wind, a whisper
where are you from?
and once more I'm on a frozen lake, crying.
I am empty,
can see no shore,
nothing sure,
I have only your stories and scripts –
such fragile foundations for
the ice is fracturing.
All I know is
where you were
was home.
Was home
where you were?
All I know is
the ice is fracturing –
such fragile foundations for
I have only your stories and scripts,
nothing sure,
can see no shore.
I am empty
and once more I'm on a frozen lake crying,
where are you? *From*
everywhere – I hear it in the wind. A whisper.

Mother's Child

Mother is a sea-fish, goes deep without knowing
how deep, to her it is natural, it is home.
In her dark places Mother dreams in colour.
When I ask how she swims through deep dark waters,
she says, *My! what difficult questions you ask, Child.*

Mother doesn't know she's a fish.
She is born of people who swam the Atlantic,
braved high seas, carried on currents and tides,
ended up on foreign silt, greeted
by blue butterflies the size of a hand,
cornflower ribbons in the air.
Mother likes ribbons and bows.
Once she gave me a ribboned dress
and I refused to wear it.
Oh my! You're not like me, Child.

Mother knows some fish fly. She fears flying,
has no wish to try lest a pelican scoops her,
swallows her whole; she keeps deep out of sight.
When I tell her the dilution of salt
in the sea is four times the strength of tears,
she says, *Child, the things you think of!*

When Mother is still, the century palms
look more vivid on water than on land.
She lives in a heat-haze where nothing is clear or dry.

When I tell her this she says,
My! what nonsense you talk, Child.
And when I ask her why she never calls me
by the name she gave me, she looks puzzled,
Child is what you'll always be.

Comb

Last summer I burned all my photos. I disliked how they lie, suggest we can. The longest I can hold my breath is three lengths of the pool. That's two minutes.

I had a photo of you when you were twelve. You looked defiant. To children the old were never young. Looking at old photos is watching a film when you know the ending.

Once, I didn't know the moon hides three days a month. I still have the wooden carving you gave me of a girl holding the moon. I wanted to be her. She was pretty and blonde with a red ribbon ponytail.

My astrology chart shows I have too many mutables. I have a friend who does astrology for horses. Maybe it works for all animals. When I look into a sheep's amber eyes, I wonder about viewing the world like a convex mirror. Imagine if I could see like that. If I'd seen your defiance, locked away when you grew old and crumpled under other people's fixed or cardinal opinions. The moon doesn't show her dark side. Maybe defiance is something I can acquire, like buying honey in a supermarket.

You gave me your hairbrush when you started using a comb. It was tortoiseshell. You let me have a tortoise. I called it Testudo. It liked to hide in its shell.

When I had my babies, the dog chewed the hairbrush you gave me. We were visiting friends with babies. The dog found their tortoise hibernating. I caught the dog tossing their tortoise to the moon. When you broke your tortoiseshell comb, you used one half, said it was enough.

Your house grew cold. When I visited, I felt under a spell, couldn't stop yawning. I wondered if I'd ever heard you laugh like you were really laughing. You were Pisces, liked dreaming. You would gaze at the moon as if she belonged to you.

The art of daydreaming

My mother gazes beyond the garden,
a capuchin in the rhododendron,
she hears tree frogs in the ticking
of the grandfather clock. My mother
has sugar-cane blood, is made of mango,
she is pineapple, dresses in laughter,
passes darkness to her big-boned
daughter to wear. Sometimes
my beautiful mother sings as she peels
potatoes. Her voice is *alto*. When she tries
soprano she's a spider monkey.
My beautiful mother's rings are loose
on her fingers, she believes rubies
and gold will bring her good luck,
she likes to lose herself in dreams.

And had I not gone to that Almodóvar film
(that I didn't enjoy) I'd have answered
her call. Not heard her voice later, too late
to return, naming me in her sing-song way
as if saying goodbye. Sometimes
we just get it wrong. That night I was
too big-boned dumb. By next morning
my beautiful mother is wading back to
childhood, ankle-deep in warm rain.

My mother is an Amazonian waterlily afloat
on dark water, her petals unfurl
like paper decoration. She doesn't see
the caiman's amber eyes waiting,
a green anaconda dangling from a branch,
the harpy eagle that'll soar her to the canopy's
green mantle. My mother doesn't like green.
Her breathing is the ocean. She is rushing in
to pause on the Demerara silt-shore,
then rushing out to rejoin the horizon,
her waves are thrashing the seawall,
she's wearing foam-lace, ribboning the air
with clouds that shapeshift, are turning
electric blue. My butterfly mother is sky.

The sea is sleeping

When I wake in the night, I see a black mirror.
I'm standing by the Georgetown seawall.
In the waves I hear you breathing. I'm thinking
about the stories we make of our lives,
if even facts can be shifted. My broken
family, all that ever matters is the heart:

constitutionals in the Botanic Gardens
picking fresh grass for the manatees;
feeding your hen, your pet monkey.
Rosa held your hand as rioters torched houses,
yours was spared out of their love for *Daddy*.
Seven father-orphans in grandmother's care.
At school you were charity. You were all so poor,
your mother abroad. They left food at your door.
When invited to a Government House party
you made your dress from a curtain.

On your father's headstone the word *regretted*
bled like a heart. Anger, fire in the heart.
Sadness, a drowning heart.
When you died your brain was still bleeding.
And the waves drew back, exposing the silt.

Daisy ring

I never knew its provenance, never saw her wear it,
but that day we divided up her jewellery
I took a ring, old yet new, held it to the light.

A daisy head of seven diamonds, sparkling, as she
craved the sun and colour, as if afraid of night.
I never knew its provenance, never saw her wear it.

O, the tales she would magic to us of her colonial past,
her childhood where bad things never happened.
I took this ring, old yet new, held it to the light.

My sisters urged me to hurry as I wrestled with choice,
tempted by the more familiar amethyst, rubies, gold –
I never knew its provenance, never saw her wear it.

Unguarded, she would have a hooded, silent look,
or I'd hear her sing, her voice soft and low.
I took her ring, turned it, held it to the light,

slipped it on, a perfect fit, my mother's *solis oculus*,
her petals furled at dusk, containing what we cannot know.
I never knew its provenance, never saw her wear it,
but I'll wear her ring, shining new, hold it to the light.

The Canal du Midi where I find my mother

At first she's a road
edged by plane trees
then she's lying still
her waters clouding
as boats leave
their wake & diesel fumes
mix with suncream
to create her smell.
Her colour is of weak tea
with hundreds & thousands
scattered on a party cake.
Her silence absorbs
the cast of fishing lines
& chugging motorboats
that send her slopping
to the bank
causing ducks to quack.
She yearns to be organic
like the river
crossing beneath her
can't see the Aude has
no more to offer than her.
Moorhens lead their chicks
to feed on her algae.
Black bees buzz from yellow
iris to purple clover,
dragonflies skim her skin
& perch make circles
like silent tolling
for the plane trees
bleeding, succumbing.

Simon Maddrell

Simon Maddrell was born in the Isle of Man in 1965 and raised in Bolton. After twenty years in London, he moved to Brighton & Hove in 2020.

He has been published in thirteen anthologies and diverse publications such as *AMBIT, Butcher's Dog, Stand, The New European, Morning Star, Brittle Star, The Dawntreader, Perverse, Long Poem Magazine*. Simon was longlisted for the Winchester Poetry Prize, 2021. In 2020, he was first runner-up in the Frogmore Poetry Prize, and longlisted for The Rialto Nature and Place Competition and Poetry London Mentoring Scheme.

Simon's debut pamphlet, *Throatbone,* was published by UnCollected Press and *Queerfella* jointly-won The Rialto Open Pamphlet Competition 2020.

There was a hole

in the sole of my trainer.

Mum walked out on Dad that January.
I thought it was our fault.

I wore my trainers all the time.
I was nine and school didn't care.

Summer holidays were so full of cricket
our ball fell apart at the seams.
I flattened its four parts out
and used one for the sole of my shoe.

I don't know when I got a hole in the other
but it was wet & winter.

When I told Dad he just looked.
We drove to the shop to buy new shoes.
He never asked me why I hadn't told him.

I visited Mum in her bedsit.
One wall was full of shoe boxes.
I counted them. There were fifty-two.

Only a Mother can look with

stop being difficult eyes
you're just like your father eyes
i love how fast you drive eyes
i've never liked cats, eyes
i love a bit of double entendre eyes
do you take it both ways eyes
to the pure all things are pure eyes
i wish you were a doctor eyes

only a Mother can hear with
ears that see two hundred miles
a skill i learnt from ten thousand
no, you stay there, i'm fine now
i knew yours were blinking, eyes

Alright really

After I told her, she said
*anyway, there's one at work
and he's alright really.*

She grew out of it. After
my brother died, she told me
how lovely that nurse George was.

In the 90s, she posted me
hand-written notes on
(homophobic) cartoons saying,

I thought you might like this,
and I did, not just because
they were alright really.

In the 70s, she used to say
*they pick their noses and wipe it
on the food in the market,*

so when she flirted with Kamil
during Sunday lunch, I knew
it was alright really.

If she could read this, she'd
tell me not to mock her,
I know exactly what

*you're up to, don't think
for one minute I don't,* and
I would know, it was alright really.

She never came unannounced

but that afternoon the door knock did
mums don't need to ask to sit, but she did
crouch on a dining chair in the lounge
mums don't need to ask to speak, but she did
punch memories out with her truth
splattered around the hearth.
In 1938, not 1992, the teacher spotted
the blood running on the playground
draining its way from her head with a hole
the shape of a mother's left stiletto heel.
The evacuee sent on a long country vacation,
her baby sister left behind — both collecting
a stash of happy childhoods for future masquerades.
Innocence flushed out of the cracks
after being dropped on the pavement outside her home
— a welcome mat face-down behind a locked door —
leaving a child seamstress in Shoreditch triangle.
An unreconstructed jigsaw
littered with war's holes, open wounds at home
a sweatshop with a girl in the owner's attic.
Mum hid in a raincoat on the street corner
handing out sweets & magazines
just for that one little girl too young to remember her sister
until their mother banned glossies & gobstoppers for free.
After all those bells & lemons of sixteen years
self-sacrifice from London Bridge seemed a duty
faltering, she landed in Holloway instead.
Released, she devoted herself to fifty years of nursing.

Mums don't need to ask to sit, but she did
crumple on four wooden legs like
a blackbird broken as the evening
chased the sun to the moon. Then
there was a stillness, and a song.

Rabbit-shocked

Leaving at midnight with Penny (the Lurcher, not the
Mother) with headlamp, car battery & bailing string
spotting rabbits until one freezes the lamp's gaze.

Nearly 3am and six startled eyes run around the field,
the rabbit escapes.

Penny wanted to sleep, as nothing was going to die soon
the Mother's nurse advised him to leave the green floors
& curtains and to grab a torch & batteries for his flight.

At 3am along a remote Manx road
Death hits a rabbit with its offside headlight.

Back home, he slits the unlucky rabbit pit to throat,
an errant knife spills bile over a life not yet ready,
its innards grasped and dropped to the side.

At 3am along a remote Kenyan road
News hits a man with the death of his Mother.

Back home, he peels the gutted rabbit, rolls it in flakes
of salt, its head now enclosed, skin hanging, like
a Mother's fur coat, its warmth for someone else.

At 3am the death of the Mother was nothing natural
like being hunted by a cancerous lamp.

Back in the ward, a doctor, too tired even to drive,
pushed more relief than her pain could take.

Back in a room, the man kissed her red lipstick,
a familiar taste laid out in heroin chic.

Penny

i.m. Kathleen Patricia (Penny) Maddrell

A dark African night
    pierced by an alien ship.
The moon cracked open
    with a rattled breath.

That last lingering look
    past the ice-green curtain.
A cardiac rock grief-split
    the belly, a desert hollow.

The lady at the opera
darkened lipstick washed
    indigo-lipped kiss
white-faced Penny, our Mum.

    That's Kathleen Patricia.

The lady in the morgue
darkened records washed
    opium-lipped kiss
white-faced Mum, our Penny.

Their last living look, long
    past their bedside guilt
    her cardiac rock lung-split.
The green-cloaked death secrets

    on a dark Somerset ward.
Pierced by a fatal drip
    the moon promise cracked
    with a rattled breath.

Kipper

The doctor and his witness greet me
with a pair of kippered hands
convention dictates he alone cat-whispers
go home and start the grieving process
you won't find anything here
after he fired mum's medical notes
a dead herring full of rotting smoke
my ears smelt of his guilt for nine years.

They led me down that same alley
with white walls and the same gutters
where we met before, the truth let go
exploding into brick walls, turning
into brick walls & gaslights, burning
like toast in a double-yolked slice.

Elegy

after Fiona Moore

I'm still waiting for someone
to ask, *was she murdered then?*
Of course, she was only killed
but still died before she should.
She was visited by a man late
at night with a needle he threaded
the last stitch in her blanket.
His identical twin popped by later,
with a tall cloak, a black-holed face
deep as a volcano's throat.

The church's oak creaks into silence

the carnation sea already pink
mother carried in a ship of griefs
leaking on a stained aisle carpet
speckled with stained glass sun.

The organ plays its satanic hymn
self-appointed saints jostle in pews
brass faith in a stone-faced tower
dirty water churns in an empty font.

The eulogy spills over rows of wood
dark suits weep on rose-printed tissues
as if anyone cares for badly-drawn ties
& pinholes where poppies never die.

An orphan's cup smells of bitter almonds
brown-fringed lilies held on a broken swing.

Acknowledgements

Vasiliki Albedo

'Therapy Cat' was shortlisted in the Tongues & Grooves Prose Poem Competition 2018 and included in the winners' anthology.

'Mother in fur' was longlisted for Mslexia's Single Poem Competition 2019. A previous version of 'Pine Summit' appeared in The Writer's Café magazine, *Landscapes and Maps*. 'Hard-boiled' was shortlisted for The Bridport Prize 2018. 'Last day' was shortlisted for The Bridport Prize 2021, under a different title.

Mary Mulholland

The art of daydreaming' won The Poetry Society Members' Competition, Spring 2021 and was published in *Poetry News*, Spring 2021. A previous version of 'Daisy Ring' was shortlisted for The Bridport Prize 2016 and published in *Coldweather Anthology 2017*. A previous version of 'The Canal du Midi where I find my mother' was shortlisted for The Bridport Prize 2014.

Simon Maddrell

'She never came unannounced' appeared in AMBIT 244, July 2021. 'The church's oak creaks into a silence' appeared in Atrium Poetry on Sept. 7th 2020. Previous versions of 'Alright Really' and 'There was a hole' appeared in the pamphlet *Queerfella* (The Rialto, Dec. 2020).

Lightning Source UK Ltd.
Milton Keynes UK
UKHW011817130122
397085UK00002B/130